EMOTIONAL INTELLIGENCE

And Its Association With Working Environmental Factors And Spiritual Intelligence Among Doctors

DR. NEONG SHUET CHING
DR. ZALEHA MD ISA
DR. MOHD RIZAL BIN ABDUL MANAF

INDIA • SINGAPORE • MALAYSIA

ISBN 979-8-89632-756-1

CHAPTER 1

INTRODUCTION

Multiple intelligences, according to Gardner is the product based on the belief that a person possesses other intelligences other than the traditional Intelligence Quotient (IQ) (Conti & Holly 2018). Gardner developed this theory in 1983, which serves the purpose to provide an explanation and outlook to how the mind works, and not educational in purpose. Gardner in originality defined multiple intelligences as consisting of seven types of intelligences, i.e. linguistic, logical-mathematical, musical, bodily-kinesthetic, spatial, intrapersonal, and interpersonal. Linguistic intelligence depicts the capability of an individual to use language as a means of learning and thinking. These might be suitable for those in the careers of writing, teaching, and law. There are three intelligences which are associated with art. These are musical, bodily-kinesthetic, and spatial intelligence. These are suitable for those pursuing a career in arts, dance, and theatre. Lastly, the other two intelligences are intrapersonal and interpersonal intelligences. Interpersonal intelligence is the capability to discern the desires, feelings, and motivations of other people. Intrapersonal intelligence is the understanding of one's self (Conti & Holly 2018). The constructs of these personal intelligences, which are interpersonal and intrapersonal intelligence are closely tied to the profession of a doctor.

These constructs also mirror the criteria of emotional intelligence (Bay & Lim, 2006).

It was noted that the popular interest in emotional intelligence comes from a perspective which is cross-fertilised by academic studies. These studies gained its trajectory to develop its theories sophisticatedly from psychological and biological concomitants, causes, and antecedents of emotionally intelligent behaviours. The concept of emotional intelligence did not magically appear out of the blue. According to Gardner, if he was right in his time, we will no longer refer to individuals as being more or less intelligent than others. Instead, we will be referring to some as more highly functioning compared to others in certain activities, while some may function at a lower level compared to others. The term emotional intelligence has been attributed to various sources. In terms of scientific psychology, references has been made to German psychologist, Barbara Leuner, who first elaborated on emotional quotient in 1966. Then Wayne Payne in 1966 argued that emotional awareness among children is an important concept in children development. However, it was only in 1993 that Jack Mayer and Peter Salovey featured the first systematic review on emotional intelligence. In 1995, it was followed by the elaboration of the concept of emotional intelligence by Daniel Goleman (Zeidner, Matthews & Roberts 2009).

Based on literature, in 1990s, Mayer and Solovey drew a link between Gardner's theory of multiple intelligences and the development of the term emotional intelligence as we understand it today. Literature goes to show that there is a linkage between interpersonal intelligence and intrapersonal intelligence with emotional intelligence. According to current literature, these two personal intelligences are also deemed as emotional intelligence as we undersand it today (Bay & Lin 2006).

The current term of emotional intelligence is described as a "constellation of emotional perceptions" (i.e. trait emotional intelligence) or "a set of skills to process emotionally related information" (Walter, Shenaar-Golan & Routray 2021; Mayer & Salovey 1997; Mayer et al. 2001). In alternative terms, emotional intelligence refers to the ability of individuals to make a link between the emotions that they feel and come up with reasonings which enable them to guide their actions and as a loop effect, use the reasonings to guide their emotions (Walter, Shenaar-Golan & Routray 2021; Mayer et al. 2001). Emotional intelligence, has long been attributing and is a predictor of well-being in a doctor (Walter, Shenaar-Golan & Routray 2021; Davidson, Jackson & Kalin 2000). Well-being is traditionally measured subjectively using its cognitive and affective components. This is denoted by the presence of positive affect and absence of negative affect (Walter, Shenaar-Golan & Routray 2021; Schimmack 2008).

The perception, management, and utilisation of emotional intelligence skills is deemed necessary in predicting success of a doctor's career (Ravikumar et al. 2017). This is apart from Intelligence Quotient (IQ), which has traditionally been deemed to be of utmost important in determining a doctor's success path. There are six core competencies according to the Accreditation Council for Graduate Medical Education (ACGME) which are patient care, system-based practice, professionalism, interpersonal and communication skills, medical knowledge, and practice-based learning. All these can be achieved if an individual possesses high IQ, intrapersonal intelligence, and interpersonal intelligence as denoted by Gardner above. As these personal constructs are closely tied to emotional intelligence, thus, we can see the correlation between personal intelligence and emotional intelligence (Ranasinghe et al. 2017; Arora et al 2010).

STUDY BACKGROUND

In literature, perceived stress is signified by a degree to which one's life is deemed as stressful. Doctors are often deemed as primary level caregivers in a hospital institution, and this often leads to stress-induced morbidities and dissatisfaction, which will indirectly cause reduced patient satisfaction with the particular doctor (Thomas 2004). If this is left unattended, it will create a loop effect, in which the doctor will accumulate more stresses as time passes, which will cause burnout in the individual in long term. Burnout is an effective state of emotional, mental, and physical exhaustion as a response to long-term stress. Burnout consists of three components, which are physical fatigue, cognitive weariness, and emotional exhaustion (Mitra et al. 2018; Shirom 2003).

Burnout has long been shown to be common among doctors. Burnout will affect the physical and mental health of doctors, which further impedes their performance and provision of quality of care. In the study by Khoo et al. (2017), it was shown that high and moderate emotional exhaustion has been reported by 25.4% and 24.4% of doctors respectively, and there is a significant association between burnout and stress among doctors. The components of stresses come from dealing with patient's psychosocial problems, a lack of respect among fellow doctors and subordinates, lack of appreciation shown by immediate supervisors, lack of promotions and incentives, time pressures and deadlines to meet, coming up with unrealistic goals to achieve by oneself, and dealing with difficult parents, all of which will only be exacerbated during the dealing with pandemic Covid-19.

The combination of stress and burnout may produce an effect on patient care and performance. There is an absolute correlation between emotional intelligence and stress as shown by Yildirim-Hamurcu & Terzioglu (2021). This study is one of the latest studies to show correlations between emotional intelligence in health care workers, and stresses perceived by individuals. The study goes on to show that "assignments and workloads" as well as "taking care of patients" as the highest sources of stresses experienced by clinician health care workers (Yildirim-Hamurcu & Terzioglu 2021).

Starting from December 2019 to present, COVID-19 has proven to be a devastating pandemic which affects the whole world. As such in Malaysia, the recent waves of COVID-19 affecting the country has toppled the healthcare system and proves to be a major stressor in the country (Abbas et al. 2021). As a result of the COVID-19 pandemic, there is evidence of excessive work stress among health care workers throughout the world. A study by Abbas et al. (2021) has shown that there is an association between pandemic and the stress caused by it among health care workers, and at the same time there is no wholesome climate to reduce the stresses experienced by health care workers.

However, despite the events of stressful situations, the existence of self-efficiency in an individual doctor to perceive, grasp the understanding, and manage own's and others' emotions, and be able to adapt and cope successfully with his or her surroundings, whether it being internal or external surrounding, is termed emotional intelligence (Mitra et al. 2018; Satterfield, Swenson & Rabow 2009).

Thus, during this time, it depends on the individual's emotional intelligence ability, apart from an implementation of a healthy working environment provided by supervisors which would prove effective in reducing the impact of the pandemic and perceived stress experienced by the healthcare workers. It is noted that the increased stress caused by the pandemic will prove to be more challenging and lethal compared to the pandemic itself (Abbas et al. 2021). This form of stress can lead to emotional exhaustion, which is a key component of burnout.

PROBLEM STATEMENT

Emotional intelligence has been recognised in recency as it is highly associated with impact on organisation, human interactions, and relations. It is thus recognised as important as intelligence quotient in navigating effective response to the challenges of life (Puliyakkadi et al. 2020). The perception, management, and utilisation of emotional intelligence skills is deemed necessary in predicting success of a doctor's career (Ravikumar et al. 2017). Studies have been done to show that the average emotional intelligence of doctors tend to hover around 120 according to the Schutte Self-Report Emotional Intelligence Test (SSEIT). It is noted that this score is somewhat an average score of emotional intelligence. However, this score is much lower than the emotional intelligence scores as depicted by nursing faction and that of radiation therapists (Puliyakkadi et al. 2020; Shahid & Adams 2020; Hajibabaee et al. 2018; Ravikumar et al. 2017; Issue & Tomar 2016; Imran et al. 2013).

A doctor's career is constantly filled with stressful situations, and this is more so evident in the career of a resident-in-training. These residents work long hours, are constantly under immense academic pressure, and have the lives of others dependable on them as they work through their training. These doctors carry huge responsibility, yet with little autonomy of high degree of personal, interpersonal, and work-home interference (Mitra et al. 2018).

As it is noted, the emotional intelligence among doctors is lower than other health care workers such as nurses and radiation therapists, thus interventions are studied to improve the emotional intelligence among doctors. The introduction of work hour restrictions for residents has revealed a positive impact on the emotional intelligence among doctors, with an increase in self-perceived wellness, reduction in burnout, fatigue and physiological distress (Papanagnou 2020; Salles, Liebert & Greco 2015).

Papanagnou et al. (2020) on a study in the USA reported that the emotional intelligence of Postgraduate Year 2 (PGY-2) doctors to be lower than the Postgraduate Year 1 (PGY-1) doctors, suggesting that there is not much of emotional intelligence training in the medical curriculum. A positive linear relationship between emotional intelligence and training was not observed in this cohort. The differences of emotional intelligence scores was not found to be significant. However, a statistical significant difference was observed between the scores of PGY-2 and PGY-3 doctors. It is noted that the second year Emergency Medicine resident was expected to evaluate a larger volume of patients, in order to obtain a higher level of medical knowledge, together with caring for critically-ill patients with a marked elevated level of responsibility. Literature has suggested that caring for severely ill and critically ill patients have a negative toll on a doctor's emotional and physical well-being (Papanagnou 2020; Faye et al. 2011; Strote et al. 2011; Knazik et al. 2003; Bruce 2002).

Based on the findings of literature, it is noted that doctors-in-training may be struggling with self-expression and self-perception. One has to consider the lack of emotionally-related training in the medical curriculum as has been depicted by literature (Papanagnou 2020; ACPonline.org 2013; Crawford et al. 2010). One has to weigh in and take into account while some supervising physicians might nurture an environment which supports debate and discussion, there are others that might opt for a less supportive environment (Bounds et al. 2013). Finally, a trainee might struggle with self-expression in view of demanding clinical, professional and academic requirements in order to succeed in the medical field (Papanagnou 2020).

In other studies in India, it is noted that the emotional intelligence scores of senior doctors are higher than their junior counterparts. This is consistent with findings from another study by Issue & Tomar (2016). The reason behind this observation is associated with the literature that as one ages, one is able to better express and control oneself emotionally, where one becomes more socialised and less emotional (McCrae et al 2000; McKinley 2014; Zeidner et al. 2013; Faye et al. 2011; Weng et al. 2008). In support with the findings by Papanagnou (2020), doctors in the clinical department where doctors deal with patients are found to be less emotionally intelligent compared to their counterparts in administration (Puliyakkadi et al. 2020).

Another study by Shahid & Adams (2020) showed that doctors or residents who took a gap year seemed to show better emotional intelligence scores compared to their counterparts who did not take a gap year in between. They scored better in interpersonal skills, empathy, decision making, and impulse control. This could be because a gap year induces time for personal reflection, can inculcate maturity, helps develop one as a person, increase one's self-confidence, teaching interactions with multi-cultural society, and can help develop one's communication skills.

For example, Stanford University has provided their Balance in Life Program, which offers residents mentorship and leadership training, providing residents with healthy snacks and foods, and help residents foster a healthier mental, emotional, and physical health as well as providing social support in the forms of hosting social gatherings and events (Wire.ama-assn.org 2015). Attention should be given to trainees to increase stress tolerance, assertiveness and optimism in order to promote a culture of wellness and develop resilient trainees. From the Papanagnou study, it is noted that Postgraduate Year 3(PGY-3) doctors demonstrated the highest emotional intelligence scores. This correlates with the theory of age and training, which suggests that the residency training may have a positive effect in overall emotional intelligence development (Papanagnou 2020).

From the studies conducted worldwide, there seems to be an emphasis on emotional intelligence and its association with job satisfaction, ability to deal with stress, and job performance. As such, there is an association between poor emotional intelligence among doctors and stress in workplace. Emotional intelligence thus has been factored out as one of the interventions to improve in order to deal with these stresses that doctors have to go through.

CHAPTER 2

LITERATURE REVIEW

INTRODUCTION

The concept of emotional intelligence is perhaps still relatively novel in the field of psychology. As explained in the introduction section above, the ideas and concepts which determine the context of emotional intelligence first came to be in the 1980s, when Gardner first introduced his theory of multiple intelligences. From that, it is noted that there were two types of intelligences which are closely knitted with emotional intelligence, and these are interpersonal intelligence and intrapersonal intelligence. It is then further introduced into psychological world by Peter Salovey and John Mayer in a 1990 research paper. Only in 1995, the publication of Daniel Goleman's Emotional Intelligence: Why It can Matter More than IQ managed to popularise the concept of emotional intelligence (Wicks et al. 2021).

Emotional intelligence is described as a "constellation of emotional perceptions" (i.e. trait emotional intelligence) or "a set of skills to process emotionally related information" (Walter, Shenaar-Golan & Routray 2021; Mayer & Salovey 1997; Mayer et al. 2001). In alternative terms, emotional intelligence refers to the ability of individuals to make a link between the emotions that they feel and come up with reasonings which enable them to guide their actions and as a loop effect, use the reasonings to guide their emotions (Walter, Shenaar-Golan & Routray 2021; Mayer et al. 2001).

Emotional intelligence is also defined as an individual's capacity to identify, use, comprehend, and control emotional information which is looked upon as a critical protective resource. Emotional intelligence has also been shown to serve as a protective factor in averting psychological and behavioral disorders in children both adults and children. It can aid in the development of post-traumatic growth and more intimate interpersonal relationships. Emotional intelligence has been found to enhance the influence of another protective component (e.g., social support) and therefore, reduces stress. As per previous research, emotional intelligence can act as a moderator in the association between social support and adolescent cognition, as well as the association between stress and mental health (Ciarrochi, Deane & Anderson 2002). Emotional intelligence has been found to aid individuals in constructively coping with unfavorable external circumstances and individuals with a high level of emotional intelligence frequently experience less stress and are more likely to have increased post-trauma growth (Zhang et al. 2022).

Emotional intelligence has long been associated with burnout, job satisfaction, and work performance among resident doctors (Serebrakian et al. 2021). Emotional intelligence represents the capacity and ability to recognise and manage an individual's own emotions, and the emotions of those around him/her. This involves one's capacity of being aware of their own emotions, coupled with the ability to control their emotions. Then, they should be able to apply these emotions to different tasks (which includes thinking process and problem solving). This is followed by the ability to manage one's emotions including regulating and affecting others' emotions (Sataloff 2020). Emotional intelligence has been linked to "noncognitive attributes that help individuals perceive and regulate emotions and in turn, cope effectively with emotive situations, such as environmental stressors or interpersonal relationships," as quoted by Lin et al. (2016). Emotional intelligence has been widely associated with professional and personal success in the past two decades compared with intelligence quotient (IQ), which is the traditional way of measuring one's intelligence (Ranasinghe et al. 2017; Lopes et al. 2006; Goleman 1995).

Emotional intelligence as delineated by Mayer et al. (2008) comprises of motivation and determination, which holds a significant role in achieving goals. Higher emotional intelligence is correlated with better relationships in children and adults, better academic performance, improved relationships with colleagues, better work performance, and improved psychology well-being (Ranasinghe et al. 2017; Mayer, Roberts & Barsade 2008). Emotional intelligence is also relevant to the accounts of highly stressful working environment which doctors are constantly working in, and required to deal with (Ranasinghe et al. 2017; Evans, Goldwater & Potter 2005). The Accreditation Council for Graduate Medical Education (ACGME) in the USA has prepared and defined the six core competencies of a new doctor, which are patient care, system-based practice, professionalism, interpersonal and communication skills, medical knowledge, and practice-based learning. It is later then noted that the core competencies delineated by the ACGME were components of emotional intelligence (Ranasinghe et al. 2017; Arora et al 2010).

EMOTIONAL INTELLIGENCE THEORETICAL FRAMEWORK

There were 3 models of emotional intelligence which have been introduced, and these are namely the ability-based model, the traits model, and the mixed-method model (Table 2.1). Due to the existence of differences among the three models, there is yet a standardised definition of emotional intelligence (Wicks et al. 2021).

Table 2.1: Theoretical framework of Emotional Intelligence (Rodrigues & Robelo 2022; Punia, Dutta & Sharma 2015; O'Connor et al. 2019; Brannick et al. 2009)

Ability-based model	**Trait model**	**Mixed-methods model**
Ability-based model applies greater parameters around the constructs. This includes narrower definition, while excluding personality characteristics.	Trait model is based on the method which utilises self-report items to measure overall emotional intelligence.	Follows a more socio-emotional approach, and focus on personality characteristics.

Ability-based model	Trait model	Mixed-methods model
Refers to intellectual processing and mental aptitude, and mental abilities cannot be divorced from intellect.	Trait emotional intelligence measures typical behaviour rather than maximal performance, and thus has better grasp of actual behaviours in a range of situations.	According to Weinberger (2002), through Goleman's study within the fields of psychology and neuroscience, he described emotional intelligence as a set of traits, which culminated into an individual's character.
Emotional intelligence is an ability and a type of intelligence.	Concept based on the individual perception (assessed through self-report) about an individual's abilities to perceive, understand, regulate and use emotions to adapt to the environment and enhance well-being.	Emotional intelligence is deemed as "the capacity for recognizing our own feelings and those of others, for motivating ourselves, and for managing emotions well in ourselves and in our relationships".

Ability-based model	Trait model	Mixed-methods model
Involves appraisal and expression of emotions, regulation of emotions, and utilisation of emotions.	A good predictor of coping styles in response to stresses.	Focuses on self-awareness, self-management, social awareness, and social (relationship) management.
In 1997, Salovey and Mayer developed four branches of ability model, inclusive of 1) identifying emotions, 2) using emotions, 3) the ability to understand emotions, 4) the ability to manage emotions.	Is associated with a broad set of emotions and social-related outcomes.	Places heavy emphasis on social relationships.

Ability-based model	Trait model	Mixed-methods model
Abilities-based models apply greater parameters around emotional intelligence, including narrow definitions, and exclude many personality characteristics included in the mixed-models which create limitations with the model		Singh (2007) summarized, saying it was about self-awareness of internal feelings, self-motivation, self-creativity, and effective relationship management.
		Bar-On's Emotional-Social Intelligence (ESI) model is composed of two primary parts: (Part I) theory and (Part II) psychometric (Bar-On, 2007).

Ability-based model	Trait model	Mixed-methods model
		The theory portion provides a conceptualization, or context, to the ESI model; the psychometric portion of the model, represented by Bar-On's EQ-I (emotional quotient inventory) assessment, provides the ability to measure ESI (Bar-On 2007). Bar-On's ESI model is defined as "one's intrapersonal ability to be aware of oneself, to understand one's strengths and weaknesses, and to express one's feelings and thoughts non-destructively"

According to the performance-based ability model, emotional intelligence is viewed as part of intelligence which is based on emotional aptitudes, and is seen as a mental ability which involves reasoning about one's emotions, that is focused on hot information processing (Gutiérrez-Cobo, Cabello & Fernández-Berrocal 2017; Mayer, Caruso & Salovey 2016). Within the framework, emotional intelligence is evaluated by solving emotional problems through performance tests that include a set of correct and incorrect responses. This model is further defined in the instrument "Mayer-Salovey-Caruso Emotional Intelligence Test" (MSCEIT; Mayer, Salovey & Caruso 2002). Similar to the performance-based ability model, the self-report ability model views emotional intelligence as a combination of emotional aptitudes. However in this case, self-report instruments are utilised, where those involved need to estimate their own emotional intelligence in a subjective manner. Therefore, in this model, there are no correct or incorrect responses, of which the "Trait Meta-Mood Scale" (TMMS) being a commonly utilised instrument for this model (Gutiérrez-Cobo, Cabello & Fernández-Berrocal 2017; Fernández-Berrocal & Extremera 2008).

Trait emotional intelligence model offers a comprehensive scientific framework which is able to interpret a diverse results of independent empirical research which is consistent with individual differences in personality and emotion throughout their lifespan. Trait emotional intelligence can be viewed as a personality trait. It can be interpreted as a non-cognitive component in the measurement of emotional intelligence (Pérez-González, Saklofske & Mavroveli 2020).

The self-report mixed model does not consider emotional intelligence to be a form of intelligence, and instead depicts it as a broad concept which includes motivations, interpersonal and intrapersonal abilities, empathy, personality factors, and well-being. This model utilizes self-report instruments which evaluate the subjective perception of the participants, of which the "Bar-On Emotional Quotient Inventory of EQi is a usually used test for this model (Gutiérrez-Cobo, Cabello & Fernández-Berrocal 2017; Mayer, Roberts & Barsade 2008a).

Although there were differences between these models, their use has yielded a huge number of emotional intelligence-related outcomes, where studies have shown higher scores of emotional intelligence linked to better mental and physical health, well being and happiness, job performance, prosocial behaviour, less aggressive behaviour and substance abuse (Gutiérrez-Cobo, Cabello & Fernández-Berrocal 2017; Schutte et al. 2007).

Advocates have found that all the different models of emotional intelligence are legitimate in measuring one's emotional intelligence (Brown, Bryant & Reilly 2006).

Figure 2.1 is an elaborated representation of Daniel Goleman's model of emotional intelligence which involve four aspects of emotional intelligence; self-awareness, self-management, social awareness and relationship management. This model was originally developed in

1998, with 5 domains and was then redesigned with 4 domains in 2002. Each domain has the connected competencies as listed in Figure 2.1. It is perhaps one of the most popular model of emotional intelligence in the history of emotional intelligence definitions.

<table>
<tr><td rowspan="4">S
E
L
F</td><td colspan="2">RECOGNITION/AWARENESS</td><td rowspan="4">O
T
H
E
R
S</td></tr>
<tr><td>Self Awareness
Emotional Self-awareness
Accurate Self-assessment
Self-confidence</td><td>Social Awareness
Empathy
Organisational awareness
Service</td></tr>
<tr><td>Self-management
Emotional Self-control
Transparency
Adaptability
Achievement
Initiative
Optimism</td><td>Relationship-management
Influence
Inspirational Leadership
Developing Others
Change catalyst
Building bonds
Conflict Management
Teamwork & Collaboration</td></tr>
<tr><td colspan="2">REGULATION / CONTROL</td></tr>
</table>

Figure 2.1: Goleman's Model of Emotional Intelligence

1. SELF-AWARENESS

(Emotional self-awareness, Accurate self assessment, Self-confidence)

According to John Mayer (a psychologist in the University of New Hampshire and one of the first to investigate on emotional intelligence), self-awareness is being "aware of both our mood and our thoughts about mood". It is is further explained by Goleman in 2002, that self-awareness is the ability to read and understand one's emotions as well as recognize their impact on others. It can simply be put that self-awareness is a fundamental understanding of how and why we feel that way.

Emotional awareness is the result of this sequence:

1. Sense the emotion (feeling)
2. Acknowledge the feeling
3. Identify more facts
4. Accept the feeling
5. Reflect on why the emotion is showing up in that moment. Notice what other feelings are present or came before it. Ask yourself what its purpose might be, what it is communicating, demonstrating, or trying to teach you.
6. Act – bring your thoughts and feelings up and take appropriate action, if needed.
7. Reflect on the usefulness of the response and what lesson you would like to take away.

(Barsade 2002; Goleman 1998; Goleman, Boyatzis & McKee 2002)

2. SELF-MANAGEMENT

(Emotional Self-Control, Transparency, Adaptability, Achievement, Initiative, Optimism)

Self-management can be reported as the ability to manage an individual's actions, thoughts, and feelings with flexibility in order to get desired results. Optimal self-regulation contributes to a sense of well-being, a sense of self-efficacy or confidence, and a sense of connectedness to others. This is a self-regulatory approach for an individual to view his or her emotional responses as cues for both action and coping effectively in relationships (Barsade 2002; Goleman 1998; Goleman, Boyatzis & McKee 2002).

3. SOCIAL AWARENESS

(Empathy, Organisational awareness, Service)

Social awareness informs the ability to accurately take notice of others' emotions and read situations tangibly. This is about sensing what others are thinking and feeling, using the capacity of oneself for empathy. "Empathy refers to the cognitive and emotional processes that bind people together in various kinds of relationships that permit sharing experiences as well as understanding of others" (Eslinger 1998). There is a prerequisite of being aware of others' emotions and the circumstances surrounding them. Social awareness is all about noticing the person in the room who happens to be frustrated by the work at hand and responding in a manner which can avert further negative emotions (Barsade 2002; Goleman 1998; Goleman, Boyatzis & McKee 2002).

4. RELATIONSHIP-MANAGEMENT

(Influence, Inspirational Leadership, Developing Others, Change Catalyst, Building Bonds, Conflict Management, Teamwork & Collaboration)

Relationship-management refers to the capacity to take an individual's own emotions, as well as others' emotions and the contest to manage social interactions with success. This quadrant combines the other 3 components and creates the final product, which is relationship-management. This can also be denoted as "friendliness with a purpose" or in other words, getting the desired outcomes when working with others. This context can be used to influence the people we meet daily and make good decisions. The reactions of others are easily sensed with regards to the situation and response to the situations are fine-tuned, moving the interaction into a positive direction. An example of the application of this dimension is dealing with conflicts with others. Listening and empathizing are crucial skills to deal with these often difficult conversations. Other than these, it was also noted that relationship management can include the context of working with others and teamwork, steering into achieving the ultimate goals (Barsade 2002; Goleman 1998; Goleman, Boyatzis & McKee 2002).

EMOTIONAL INTELLIGENCE AMONG DOCTORS

☆☆☆

Many studies have been conducted to investigate the emotional intelligence among doctors. Emotional intelligence has been investigated in relations with surgeons' burnout and doctor-patient relationships. In these studies, there are proposals on improving the emotional intelligence among surgeons/ surgical residents (Abi- Jaoudé et al. 2021).

Among the studies conducted, there are various aspects of doctors' well-being which have been investigated extensively. For example, among surgical residents, there was a 60.3% of burnout rate reported, together with depersonalisation and emotional exhaustion. Other than these, there were reported rates of depression among doctors, in particular residents and practising physicians. The rate of depression among this group of doctors were reported from 22% to 50%. It was further delineated that there is a high risk of suicide in male residents age-matched and sex-matched among their peers in the general population, recording 1.5-3.8 fold greater, whereas the successful suicide rate among female residents were reported to be 3.7 to 4.5 times greater (Sataloff 2020; Lin et al. 2016; Balch, Freischlag & Shanafelt 2009; Schernhammer & Colditz 2004). From the studies, it was noted that emotional intelligence was found to be a strong predictor of residents' general well-being, and the residents with higher emotional intelligence tended to perform in their residency compared to those with lower emotional intelligence scores. There was also an association between high emotional intelligence with psychological well-being with inverse correlation with parameters of burnout including depression, depersonalisation and emotional exhaustion (Sataloff 2020; Lin et al. 2016).

There were many studies which investigated residents' burnout rate, and these studies provided observations and high incidence of burnout among their surgical residents. In one of these studies, there was an 82% of burnout in the surgical residents, with highly reported prevalence of depersonalisation and emotional exhaustion. It was noted that the burnout rate among surgical residents were higher than practising surgeons, which reported approximately 28%-48% of burnout rate (Sataloff 2020; Lin et al. 2016; Shanafelt, Balch & Bechamps 2009; Collier et al. 2002). In a review written by Sotaloff (2020) and Lin et al. (2016), it was shown that burnout rates can change with circumstances. Emotional intelligence was postulated to be possibly changed with interventions which increase emotional intelligence. In these studies, emotional intelligence was found to be the only significant predictor of burnout, psychological wellness, and depression. In the primary healthcare sector, it was reported that 1 in 2 primary health physicians experienced some sort of burnout, associated with depersonalisation and depression (Delgado et al. 2020).

Fatigue in the workplace has two constructs, i.e. both physical and mental dimensions, which carries a toll on the overall workers' well-being. Reduced proprioception and strength as a result of fatigue leads to low work performance, quality, and resulting in high incidence of accidents and human errors (Liu et al. 2018; Bérastégui et al. 2018; McClelland et al. 2017). In the long term, fatigue may result in various adverse health outcomes. Some of these include burnout, chronic fatigue syndrome, and work-related musculoskeletal disorders (Liu et al. 2018; Sadeghniiat-Haghighi & Yazdi 2015; Rose et al. 2017). Within the fraternity of medical doctors, fatigue has been described as a pertinent and serious issue. Fatigue has long been noted to be highly prevalent among doctors. As there is always a shortage of health care workers throughout the world, doctors are often overworked, and have to work in a stressful environment. Both physical and mental health of doctors are at stake when this happens. Other than these, the presence of stressors at work could lead to decline in work quality and efficiency, affecting doctor-patient relationship and directly hampers patient satisfaction in doctors' work (Lin et al. 2017; O'Donnell et al. 2015; Wada et al. 2008).

In the hospital institution, fatigue among doctors can be a result of high workload, and demanding psychological and environmental factors. In these doctors, it must be noted that it is not only physical demands that overwork these doctors, but mental construct has a place in affecting these doctors' health as well. Work stress perceived by the doctors could overwhelm them leading to negative emotions which will eventually consume them. Moreover, mental fatigue can precipitate physical fatigue. Thus, the regulation of emotions can have a role in preventing fatigue among doctors. Emotional intelligence has been cited as an important internal resource in dealing with interpersonal emotional pressure. This happens because a doctor is tasked to deal with patients and family members in the process of diagnosis and treatment. Moreover, they need to interact with people on a day-to-day basis, be it their colleagues or clients. Thus, a doctor with higher emotional intelligence are better able to cope with the work stress and able to reduce tiredness as a result of day-to-day work (Liu et al. 2018; Weng et al. 2011; Psilopanagioti et al. 2012).

Emotional intelligence, in which its concept was first proposed by Salovey and Mayer in 1990, was shown to be necessary in the processes of diagnosis and treatment, as specific and appropriate emotions in response to their patients in a highly stressful environment are exhibited (Weng et al. 2011; Psilopanagioti et al. 2012). Emotional intelligence proves to be an important resource for managing interpersonal emotional pressure when interacting with patients' family members, nurses, and fellow doctors from multidisciplinary departments. Doctors with higher emotional intelligence are more prone to release work stresses and fatigue by emotions control. A previous study by Psilopanagioti et al. (2012) has gone to show that doctors who utilized practical skills of emotional intelligence such as empathy, adaptability, confidence, and conflict resolve manage to communicate well with patients and colleagues, thus increasing patient and colleague satisfaction with their works (Liu et al. 2018; Psilopanagioti et al. 2012). As such, effective patient-doctor communication is essential in providing high quality healthcare services (GMC 2021; Maguire & Pitceathly 2002).

Highly efficient emotional intelligence and leadership traits are found to be necessary for doctors in managing their responsibilities, thus building successful interaction with patients and patients' families. A study conducted by Coskun et al. (2018) found that there is an association between emotional intelligence and doctors' sociodemographic factors. There was also an association between family doctors' emotional intelligence and leadership traits. These leadership traits are found to play significant roles in improving a physician's personal and professional development. These also increase the quality of health services rendered by the doctors, and increase caregiving competencies which in turn decrease physicians' burnout and fatigue (Coskun et al. 2018).

A study by Sharp, Bourke & Rickard (2020) went on to explain and explore the benefits of the current era's health care system, with an emphasis on the field of surgery. It is noted that individuals with higher emotional intelligence has various proposed benefits, ranging from increasing work satisfaction to reducing stress and burnout. As such, the business world recognises emotional intelligence as useful in terms of outcomes and performance. For optimal performance, doctors must be aware of their own emotions and others. Emotional intelligence is deemed different from intelligence quotient, in that emotional intelligence can be taught, learnt, and improved upon. High emotional intelligence is associated positively with leadership skills among surgeons, reduction in surgeons' stress, burnout, increased in job satisfaction, and also associated with better non-technical skills. It is suggested from this study that emotional intelligence should be a compulsary scale in surgical training among doctors (Sharp, Bourke & Rickard 2020).

A study by Papanagnou et al. (2020) has stated that physicians who are superior in expressing their emotions had been rated by patients as more sensitive, caring, and better at listening. Patient satisfaction was found to be strongly associated with emotional expressions of non-verbal behaviours (Papanagnou et al. 2020; Weng et al. 2011; Griffith et al. 2003). Physicians often encounter challenge with perceiving and responding to their emotions, as well as the emotions of their patients and multidisciplinary teams. There is a further need to understand the internal thoughts and interlacing emotions as healthcare providers are potentially able to improve healthcare services through enhanced patient care by improving on communication skills and professionalism (GMC 2021). The role of emergency physicians include but not enhaustive of, effectively communicating, empathizing with patients and families, and empathizing with care teams, co-ordinating patient care with other providers, and making holistic, expeditious decisions at the same time. Taking into consideration the degree to which emergency physicians are expected to make important decisions, develop interpersonal relationships, and manage stress effectively in the clinical context of Emergency Department, the role of emotional intelligence in developing a successful career cannot be taken lightly (Papanagnou et al. 2017).

Doctors suicide has proven to be a major challenge for the medical fraternity, and as many studies have delineated, residents are not spared from this tragedy. Emotional intelligence as mentioned above, has time and time again been shown to be essential in coping with stress, as well as to creating a more wholesome well-being in doctors' physical and mental capacity. It is therefore only timely that the intersection of emotional intelligence, mental health, and coping abilities underscores the importance of increased understanding of residents' emotional intelligence. There should be a better understanding in order to promote and inform educational wellness interventions among residents (Papanagnou et al. 2017; Matthew & Zeidner 2001; Ciarrochi, Dean & Anderson 2002).

Many studies, which were done between 2014 to 2017, have included investigations of emotional intelligence in residents of multiple disciplines including obstetrics and gynaecology, orthopaedics, otorhinolaryngology, pathology, paediatrics, general surgery, and emergency residencies. These indicate potential training interventions which may be appropriately designed to support well-being, and address emotional intelligence. The authors continued to seek and reveal findings which could potentially affect direct future residency training, development of curriculum, and educational programming in order to address residents' self-awareness and efficacy (Papanagnou et al. 2017; Ogunyemi et al. 2014; Chan, Petrisor & Bhandari 2014; Dugan et al. 2014; McKinley et al. 2015).

There are many factors which affect the emotional intelligence in doctors. There are the personality traits, and social factors, which are made constant in this study by accounting for confounders. There are also sociodemographic factors which have been shown to exert their effects on emotional intelligence of healthcare workers in general, and doctors in specific. Other than these are what we term the environmental factors which encompass organizational culture, spiritual intelligence, cultural competence and cultural awareness, which have been shown to affect doctors' emotional intelligence scores.

ORGANISATIONAL CULTURE AND EMOTIONAL INTELLIGENCE

☆☆☆

Health systems reforms starting from the early 2000s tended to primarily focus on structural reforms. This include the introduction of managed care, the establishment of governing bodies of international clinical practice guidelines, the implementation of a medication error reporting system, and the restructuring of primary care. However, it is noted that these are not sufficient to ensure that healthcare delivery runs at an optimal state. Thus, we hear calls to implement and transform organisational culture in workplace, in order to deliver changes in quality and performance (Zeb et al. 2021; Scott et al. 2003; Hutchison, Abelson & Lavis 2001).

Organisational culture is made up of the fundamental values, assumptions, and beliefs which were held in common by members of an organisation. This social construct is stable, and is subconscious, where employees are deemed to impart the organisational culture to new staff, and this culture plays an important role in how employees relate to one another, and their work environment. Theorists further propose that organisational culture is one of the most critical, if not the most, in disseminating new knowledge and implementing new technical innovations (Zeb et al. 2021; Helfrich et al. 2007; Ostroff, Kinicki & Tamkins 2003). Organisational culture has been shown to provide basic values, beliefs and principles which act as a fundamental ground for an organisation's management system, as well as to the practical and behavioural management components which demonstrate and strengthen those foundations, which then determine an individual's or a group's actions, thinking, values, and perceptions (Aydogdu & Asikgil 2011; Martins & Coetzee 2007).

Health services researcher more commonly used the Quinn and Rohrbaugh's Competing Value Framework (CVF) in order to assess an organisation's culture and also linking it with important indicators of healthcare processes and outcomes (Zeb et al. 2021; Adams, Dawson & Foureur 2017). Thus, researchers have often associated organisational culture to creating important differences among healthcare facilities in organisational performance, quality improvement implementation, patient care quality, efficiency, effectiveness of provider teams, job satisfaction among its health care workers, and last but not least, patient satisfaction (Zeb et al. 2021; Adams, Dawson & Foureur 2017; Gifford, Zammuto & Goodman 2002; Goodman, Zammuto & Gifford 2001).

According to the Competing Value Framework, there are four types of organisational cultures. These are :

1. Clan culture (internal focus and flexible), with a friendly workplace where leaders act like father figures.
2. Adhocracy culture (external focus and flexible), where it is a dynamic workplace with leaders that stimulate innovation.

3. Market culture (external focus and controlled), where it is a competitive workplace with leaders like hard drivers.
4. Hierarchy culture (internal focus and controlled), where it is a structured and formalised workplace and managers act like coordinators.

(Mahran 2016)

Organisational culture was first studied in management science around the end of the twentieth century, of time when the Japanese companies dictate changes in drivers' environment, which then directs the attention of researchers to study the organisational culture (Mahran 2016). There was a study conducted in Saudi Arabia, where it was aimed to investigate the impact of organisational culture on employee performance, and it was shown that some fundamental principles dictate organisational performance and affect power distance, individualism, masculinity and uncertainty avoidance. As a matter of fact, organisational culture has assisted in accounting for the limitations to overcome the measurement of performance. It is further noted that there is a negative correlation beween the culture and the performance of a staff. Thus, from these studies, it is noted that there is an important role in creating quality healthcare, which embodies the six fundamental components of quality, i.e. timeliness, effectiveness, efficacy, patient centred, safety, and equitable (Mahran 2016; Domnariu, Cernuşcă-miţariu & Boitan 2013).

Organisations which are deemed more emotionally intelligent, can increase emotional intelligent behaviours among its employees and collective ability. Managing organisational culture necessitates deeper relationship management in order to produce favourable behaviour from employees (Ugoani 2015). The ability to manage emotions in relationships will allow the emotionally intelligent manager to understand employee needs and react to the actions accordingly. However, it is stated that the applicability of EI in organisational culture equilibrium requires authenticity. Authenticity is defined as "the honest expression" of internal feelings subject to sensitive consideration of others' particular needs, well-being and abilities. On the other hand, a perception of an organisation which manipulates its employees' emotions can lead people to reject others' words and behaviours. This results in a reduction or complete lack of attention. Other than authenticity, hope is also a fundamental value of emotional intelligence for managers to demonstrate during times of organisational culture architecture. Hope is realistic, and not blind when managers implement significant actions in order to build better future for the organisation and its employees. It is found that hope buffers against apathy and depression, and strengthens employees' capacity to persist under adversity (Ugoani 2015; Gardner & Stough 2002).

CULTURAL COMPETENCE, CULTURAL AWARENESS, AND EMOTIONAL INTELLIGENCE

Cultural competence education for healthcare professionals have one common aim, which is to ensure all people receive effective health care, equitable services, particularly those from culturally and linguistically diverse (CALD) backgrounds. Health behaviour was deemed to improve significantly comparatively to controls. Other than these, involvement in care by the non-Western patients with largely Western doctors was seen to improve in terms of mutual understanding (Drame et al. 2021; Brottman et al. 2020; Horvat et al. 2014). The concept of cultural competence builds on fundamental understanding of earlier concepts such as cultural awareness, cultural security, cultural respect, and cultural safety, extending this to facilitating changes in all dimensions of practice (Horvat et al. 2014).

For the purposes of the review of cultural competence among health care workers (Drame et al. 2021), the set definition used for cultural competence is as by Cross et al. (1989). "Cultural and linguistic competence is a set of congruent behaviours, attitudes, and policies that come together in a system, agency, or among professionals that enables effective work in cross-cultural situations. 'Culture' refers to integrated patterns of human behavior that include the language, thoughts, communications, actions, customs, beliefs, values, and institutions of racial, ethnic, religious, or social groups. 'Competence' implies having the capacity to function effectively as an individual and an organization within the context of the cultural beliefs, behaviours, and needs presented by consumers and their communities" (Cross 1989).

An association between culture, language and patient safety outcomes has been demonstrated and there exist health disparities and poorer quality of care when healthcare workers fail to address the issue of culture, ethnicity and language in the provision of healthcare services (Drame et al. 2021; Horvat et al. 2014; Wilson-Stronks et al. 2008; Johnstone 2006). The review by Horvat et al. (2014) provides the best available evidence for widely used interventions with the aim of improving cultural competence among healthcare workers working with CALD populations.

In recency, there was some empirical work which has emerged that draws connections between emotional intelligence and intercultural skills, and between intercultural competence and empathy particularly (Guntersdorfer & Golubeva 2018; González Castillo et al. 2013). Studies have gone on to show that emotional intelligence can be a predictor of accounting for students' intercultural growth in the form of reduced ethnocentrism and reduced communication apprehension. It was suggested that there is a definite link between cultural competence and emotional intelligence, however the debate goes on to speculate if it is the former affecting the latter or the other way round.

A study by Drame et al. (2021) shows that the self-cultural scale (part of the cultural awareness scale) was significantly correlated to higher overall emotional intelligence scores, and a previous cultural competency training was associated with significantly higher scores on the cultural competence scale, and higher emotional intelligence score. Previous cultural competency training was also found to be associated with enhanced ability to perceive one's own emotions as measured by the emotional intelligence scale.

Other than these initial analyses, there are phrases emerging on the Internet and in smaller scale research further suggesting a little-noticed relationship. One of these is the concept of "intercultural emotional intelligence," which has yet to be further investigated, but which is beginning to be used in other factions (Guntersdorfer & Golubeva 2018; Horvat et al. 2014).

SPIRITUAL INTELLIGENCE AND EMOTIONAL INTELLIGENCE

Spirituality is perceived as an inherent dimension of human nature and is considered as the source of all feelings, values, thoughts, and behaviours of individuals. The concept of spirituality is important and this forms the basis of doctoring actions. However, there are not many studies which correlates spirituality with the caring behaviour of health care workers (Sancoko, Setiawan & Troena 2019; Kaur, Sambasivan & Kumar 2013; Hosseini et al. 2010). Spiritual intelligence is defined as "a set of mental capacities which contributes to the awareness integration, and adaptive application of the non-material and transcendent aspects of one's existence, leading to such outcomes as deep existential reflection, enhancement of meaning, recognition of a transcendent self, and mastery of spiritual states" (Sancoko, Setiawan & Troena 2019; Kaur, Sambasivan & Kumar 2013; King & DeCicco 2009).

Other than self-awareness, spiritual intelligence implies an awareness of one's relationship with the transcendent, with each other, to the earth and all beings. From the above theoretical definition of spiritual intelligence and findings in research studies, it can be concluded that spiritual intelligence is the ability of intelligence to deal with and solve problems of meaning or value, which can place behavior when dealing with fellow human beings, assessing that one's actions or way of life are more meaningful than others (Sancoko, Setiawan & Troena 2019). According to Wigglesworth (2011), spiritual intelligence is "the ability to behave with caring and wisdom while maintaining peace in (calm) and outside without regard to circumstances". The statement "without regard to circumstances" goes to show that people can relate to a center of peace and loving behavior even if faced with great pressure (Sancoko, Setiawan & Troena 2019).

From studies conducted, it was delineated that the ability of employees in terms of spiritual intelligence, can enhance and improve the emotional intelligence of these employees well. It is further concluded that the relationship between these two variables is significant. A study of emotional intelligence and employee performance and employee emotional intelligence goes to show that spiritual intelligence has a profound effect on employee performance. There is a fairly strong correlation between spiritual intelligence and emotional intelligence, and a strong correlation between spiritual intelligence and employee performance (Sancoko, Setiawan & Troena 2019; Aghajani & Samadifard 2019).

That is to say that changes in the values of spiritual intelligence through the four indicators used, namely higher self /ego self awareness, universal awareness, higher self-mastery, and social mastery / spiritual presence will be followed by impact on emotional intelligence seen from the four dimensions of Goleman's model of emotional intelligence (Sancoko, Setiawan & Troena 2019; Koohbanani et al. 2013). The findings from this study shows that spiritual intelligence, more commonly defined by a feeling which is felt and connected with oneself, others and the universe helps employees improve themselves based on the relationship of work harmony with the company (Sancoko, Setiawan & Troena 2019; Aghajani & Samadifard 2019).

SOCIODEMOGRAPHIC FACTORS AND EMOTIONAL INTELLIGENCE

☆☆☆

There is a dearth of literature researching on various factors which might navigate one's emotional intelligence. Thus, sociodemographic factors are not exempted from these investigations into emotional intelligence.

According to Papanagnou et al. (2017), mean emotional intelligence were higher in female doctors (106; 95% CI, 100-112) than male doctors (101; 95% CI, 95-108); however, there is no statistical significance in the difference of means. When examining the mean emotional intelligence scores by the year of training, those in the second year showed the lowest mean emotional intelligence score (95; 95% CI, 87-104), versus those in year 1 ((104, 95% CI, 95-114), whereas those in the third year demonstrated the highest emotional intelligence score (110, 95% CI, 103-116). The difference in means in these different levels of training is found to be statistically significant.

According to Cherry et al. (2017), there is no significant differences found in participating doctors' scores in terms of their gender, age, and ethnicity. However, there were significant negative correlations between attachment avoidance and emotional intelligence, particularly on perceiving emotions, while attachment anxiety was not found to be correlated with emotional intelligence.

There were no statistically discernable differences in emotional intelligence scores between male (n = 27) and female doctors (n = 19), or previous military experience. Female general surgery doctors show higher global emotional intelligence. Both males and females scored higher in the self-control factor than the normative population. Mid-residency, there is a non-statistically significant dip in many facets of emotional intelligence (Placek, Franklin & Ritter 2019).

Based on the findings in a study by Coskun et al. (2018), family physicians' emotional intelligence scores differ based on sex, age, health-care experience, and the geographical region where they work. Female doctors had higher mean values than men for well-being, emotionality, and global emotional intelligence scores. Physicians aged 29 years and younger had the lowest mean values for emotional intelligence. Physicians' emotional intelligence increased as they gather more healthcare experiences. Physicians working in the Mediterranean had the highest mean emotional intelligence scores. There was a positive correlation between family physicians' emotional intelligence and leadership traits. Higher emotional intelligence was correlated with increased leadership traits.

A study conducted by Sabanciogullari et al. (2019) shows that the emotional intelligence scores of the nurses were found to be higher than that of the doctors. This difference is found to be statistically significant (respectively, $t = 3.42$, $p < 0.01$; $t = 3.15$, $p < 0.01$).

According to a study done on emotional intelligence, sociodemographic factors, and leadership traits, age and years of experience had a positive correlation with emotional intelligence, whereas years of experience, gender and age and in the current position ($p = 0.026$) were found to be positively correlated with authentic leadership. The emotional intelligence total score on the other hand was found strongly and positively related to authentic leadership. The results of regression analysis on the four emotional intelligence dimensions indicated that the extent of using emotions had the strongest influence on authentic leadership ($B = 0.99$) followed by appraisal of one's emotions ($B = 0.70$) and appraisal of others' emotions ($B = 0.69$). The simple regression analysis indicated that, for every one-point increase in total emotional intelligence score, authentic leadership score increased by 0.086 (Alshammari et al. 2020).

According to a study by Haralur et al. (2019), female participants of the study recorded a marginally higher mean emotional intelligence score of 109.67 in comparison to their male counterparts, 108.10. There were independent predictors among the sociodemographic factors. These were having siblings, with a $p=0.016$, loss of parents, $p=0.002$, parents' education, $p=0.022$, and association with parents, $p=0.03$. Participants who were found to enjoy their work were also found to be associated with higher emotional intelligence scores.

Another study by Costa et al. (2021) reported that males had higher levels of self-emotion appraisal, use and regulation of emotions, while females were reported to show higher levels of other-emotions appraisal. It is further noted that age was negatively associated with use of emotions dimensions, and positively correlated with the emotional appraisal of others. However, it is also noted that both correlation coefficients were small in this study.

A study by Shahin (2020) investigated the role of stress and sociodemographic factors in affecting emotional intelligence among student nurses and student paramedics. This study goes on to show that nursing students recorded a higher emotional intelligence compared to paramedic students, thus delineating a role of departments in an individual's emotional intelligence. Both women and Saudi nationals were also found to have higher emotional intelligence.

A study done by Cassano et al. (2020) investigating on the emotional intelligence among Master degree students of nursing and midwifery reported that females showed a higher emotional intelligence mean score compared to their male counterparts. This difference is statistically significant. Age was not found to be statistically significant in this study (Cassano et al. 2020). A study by Snowden et al. also showed that women reported a higher emotional intelligence score compared to men. Snowden et al (2015) also reported that emotional intelligence tended to increase with age.

According to another study by Al Huseini et al. (2019), female gender and a high income were significant predictors of the emotional intelligence traits score. Socio economic factors were singled out as one of the more significant associations with emotional intelligence, whereby a higher socioeconomic status is associated with lower emotional intelligence score.

In another study by Stami, Ritin & Dominique (2018), it is found that radiation therapists aged between 20-39 had higher emotional intelligence compared to those aged between 40 and 69. Those with higher employment grades tend to have higher emotional intelligence scores compared to those with lower grades of employment. Lastly, female radiation therapists tend to have higher emotional intelligence scores compared to male radiation therapists.

In a separate study by Toscane-Hermosa et al. (2020), it was shown that there were significant differences of emotional intelligence traits between females and males. There is also an appreciable relationship between emotional intelligence and individual's general well-being. However, there was no relationship found between academic performance and emotional intelligence.

From all the studies delineated above, one can appreciate the role that sociodemographic factors play in determining one's emotional intelligence score. However, we must be reminded that the factors affecting emotional intelligence is not exhaustive in nature. Thus, there are many factors which can affect the emotional intelligence scores, which have not been controlled for in these studies.

CONCEPTUAL FRAMEWORK

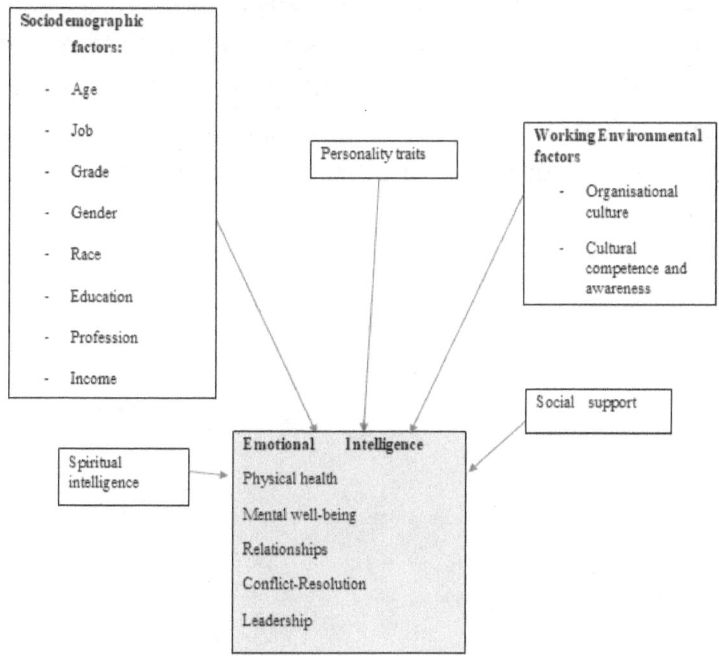

Figure 2.2: Conceptual framework of Emotional Intelligence

According to the conceptual framework in Figure 2.2 above, socio-demographic factors i.e. age, job, grade, gender, race, education, profession, income, and marital status, have been postulated to have an effect on one's emotional intelligence. Working environmental factors, such as organisational culture, cultural competence, and cultural awareness were also shown to affect an individual's emotional intelligence. Spiritual intelligence is deemed to have its effects on emotional intelligence as well. The confounders noted to have its effects on emotional intelligence are social support and personality. With the effects on these factors on emotional intelligence, one can expect a change in physical health, mental well-being, relationships, conflict resolution, and leadership, where one with higher emotional intelligence can observe a better physical health, mental well-being, better relationships with others, conflict resolution and leadership.

REFERENCES

☆☆☆

1. [www] Australian Bureau Of Statistics. 2017. Demographic Variables, 1999. Available at https://www.abs.gov.au/ausstats/abs@.nsf/Lookup/8A82CE62440E5D2DCA25697E0018FEA8?opendocument (accessed 10/11/2021)

2. [www] Current Population Estimates Malaysia, 2018. Department of Statistics Malaysia. (accessed on 25 Oct 2021)

3. [www] How one program achieved resident wellness, work-life balance. Wire.ama-assn.org. 2015 (https://wire.ama-assn.org/ life-career /how-one-program-achieved- resident-wellness-work-life-balance) (accessed 27/10/2021)

4. [www] International Encyclopedia of the Social and Behavioural Sciences, 2001. Concept of Education. Available at https://www.sciencedirect. com/topics/social-sciences/concept-of-education (accessed 10/11/2021)

5. [www] List of Hospitals in Malaysia. 2022. Available at (https://en. wikipedia.org/wiki/List_of_hospitals_in_Malaysia) (accessed 23/4/2022)

6. [www] Medical student perspective: self-expression in medicine. ACPonline.org. 2013 Available at https://www.ac-ponline.org/membership/ medical-students/acp-impact/archive/january-2013/medical-student-perspective-self-expression-in-medicine. (accessed 27/10/2021)

7. [www] Merriam-Webster Dictionary. An Encyplopedia Brittanica Company. 2021. Available at https://www.merriam-webster.com/ (accessed 30/10/2021)

8. [www] Mighty Recruiter, 2021. Job grade. Available at https:// www.mightyrecruiter.com/recruiter-guide/ hiring-glossary-a-to-z/job-grade/ (accessed 10/11/2021)

9. [www] Organisation for Economic Co-operation and Development, 2006. Glossary of Statistical Terms. Available at https://stats.oecd.org/glossary/detail.asp?ID=1597 (accessed 10/11/2021)

10. [www] The Emergency Medicine Milestone Project. ABEM.org. 2017; Available at https://www.abem.org/public/docs/default-source/migrated-documents-and-files/em-milestones.pdf?sfvrsn=6. (accessed 27/10/2021)

11. [www] World Health Organisation, 2021. Gender and Health. Available at https://www.who.int/health-topics/gender#tab=tab_1 (accessed 10/11/2021)

12. A. Ward, A. Mandrusiak, T. Levett-Jones 2018, Cultural empathy in physiotherapy students: a pre-test post-test study utilising virtual simulation Physiotherapy, 104 (4) pp. 453-461, 10.1016/j.physio.2018.07.011

13. Abbas et al, 2021. Encountering Covid-19 and perceived stress and the role of a health climate among medical workers. Curr Psychol. 1-14. doi. 10.1007/s12144-021-01381-8

14. Abdollahpour, I., Nedjat, S., Besharat, M. A., Hosseini, B., & Salimi, Y. 2016. Emotional Intelligence: A Comparison between Medical and Non-Medical Students. Iranian journal of public health, 45(2), 214–222.

15. Abe, K., Niwa, M., Fujisaki, K., & Suzuki, Y. 2018. Associations between emotional intelligence, empathy and personality in Japanese medical students. BMC medical education, 18(1), 47. https://doi.org/10.1186/s12909-018-1165-7

16. Abi-Jaoudé JG, Kennedy-Metz LR, Dias RD, Yule SJ, Zenati MA. 2021. Measuring and Improving Emotional Intelligence in Surgery: A Systematic Review. Ann Surg. doi: 10.1097/SLA.0000000000005022. Epub ahead of print. PMID: 34171871.

17. Adams, C, Dawson, A, Foureur, M. 2017. Competing Values Framework: A useful tool to define the predominant culture in a maternity setting in Australia. Women Birth 30(2): 107-113. doi. 10.1016/j.wombi.2016.09.005

18. Aghajani S, Samadifard H. 2019. Correlation of Spiritual Well-Being with Spiritual Intelligence and Emotional Intelligence in Students at Mohaghegh Ardebili University. JHPM, 8(4): 1-7

19. Agnoli, S., Mancini, G., Andrei, F., & Trombini, E. 2019. The Relationship Between Trait Emotional Intelligence, Cognition, and Emotional Awareness: An Interpretative Model. Frontiers in psychology, 10, 1711. https://doi.org/10.3389/fpsyg.2019.01711

20. Aithal A and Aithal S. 2020. Development and Validation of Survey Questionnaire Experimental Data – A Systematical Review-based Statistical Approach. MPRA Paper No. 103996

21. Akerjordet, K., & Severinsson, E. 2007. Emotional intelligence: A review of the literature with specific focus on empirical and epistemological perspectives. Journal of Clinical Nursing, 16, 1405–1416.

22. Al Huseini S et al 2019. Trait Emotional Intelligence and Its Correlates in Oman Medical Specialty Board Residents. Journal of graduate medical education, 11(4 Suppl), 134–140. https://doi.org/10.4300/JGME-D-18-00388

23. Alshammari, F., Pasay-An, E., Gonzales, F., & Torres, S. 2020. Emotional intelligence and authentic leadership among Saudi nursing leaders in the Kingdom of Saudi Arabia. Journal of professional nursing : official journal of the American Association of Colleges of Nursing, 36(6), 503–509. https://doi.org/10.1016/j.profnurs.2020.04.003

24. Antunes RR, Silva AP & Oliveira J. 2018. Spiritual Intelligence Self-Assessment Inventory: Psychometric properties of the Portuguese version of SISRI-24, Journal of Religion, Spirituality & Aging, 30:1, 12-24, DOI: 10.1080/15528030.2017.1324350

25. Appel-Meulenbroek R and Danivska V. 2021. A handbook of theories on designing alignment between people and the office environment. Routledge. New York.

26. Arnout, B. A. 2020. A structural equation model relating unemployment stress, spiritual intelligence, and mental health components: Mediators of coping mechanism. Journal of Public Affairs, 20(2), e2025.

27. Arora S, Ashrafian H, Davis R, Athanasiou T, Darzi A, Sevdalis N. 2010. Emotional intelligence in medicine: a systematic review through the context of the ACGME competencies. Med Educ. 44:749–64.

28. Austin EJ, Evans P, Goldwater R, & Potter V. 2005;. A preliminary study of emotional intelligence, empathy and exam performance in first year medical students. Pers Individ Dif. 39:1395–405.

29. Aydogdu, S., & Asikgil, B. 2011. The Effect of Transformational Leadership Behavior on Organizational Culture: An Application in Pharmaceutical Industry. International Review of Management and Marketing, 1 (4), 65-73

30. Balch CM, Freischlag JA, Shanafelt TD. 2009. Stress and burnout among surgeons: understanding and managing the syndrome and avoiding the adverse consequences. Arch Surg. 144(4):371–376.

31. Bar-On, R. (2005). The Bar-On model of emotional-social intelligence (ESI). In: P. Fernández-Berrocal & N. Extremera, Special Issue on Emotional Intelligence. Psicothema, 17(4), 1-28.

32. Bar-On, R. (2007). A broad definition of emotional-social intelligence according to the BarOn model. Retrieved from http://www.reuvenbaron.org/bar-on-model/essay.php?i=2

33. Bar-On, R. (2007). Development and validation of the Bar-On measures. Retrieved from http://www.reuvenbaron.org/bar-on-model/essay.php. IJSER

34. Bar-On, R. (2007). The conceptual aspect of the Bar-On model (the theory). Retrieved from http://www.reuvenbaron.org/bar-on-model/conceptual aspects.php

35. Bar-On, R. (2007). Theoretical foundations, background and development of the Bar-On model of emotional intelligence. Retrieved from http://www.reuvenbaron.org/bar-onmodel/essay.php.

36. Barsade, S. G. 2002. The Ripple Effect: Emotional Contagion and Its Influence on Group Behavior. Administrative Science Quarterly, 47, 644-675.

37. Bay SGK & Lim KM (2006). Correlations of Multiple Intelligences and Emotional Intelligence: A Closer Analysis of Theoretical Assumptions. The Korean Journal Of Thinking & Problem Solving 16(1), 53-64

38. Benington. 2019. Emotional Intelligence and Sociodemographic Status in Associate Degree Nursing Students. Walden Dissertations and Doctoral Studies. Walden University Scholar Works.

39. Bérastégui P, Jaspar M, Ghuysen A, Nyssen AS. 2018. Fatigue-related risk management in the emergency department: a focus-group study. Intern Emerg Med. https://doi.org/10.1007/s11739-018-1873-3.

40. Bernard HR. 2000: Social Research Methods. Qualitative and Quantitative Approaches. Thousand Oaks, CA, Sage;659.

41. Bounds R, Bush C, Aghera A, Rodriguez N, Stansfield RB, Santen S, et al 2013; Emergency medicine residents' self-assessments play a critical role when re-ceiving feedback. Acad Emerg Med. 20(10):1055-61.

42. Brannick, M. T., Wahi, M. M., Arce, M., Johnson, H. A., Nazian, S., & Goldin, S. B. (2009). Comparison of trait and ability measures of emotional intelligence in medical students. Medical education, 43(11), 1062–1068. https://doi.org/10.1111/j.1365-2923.2009.03430.x

43. Braun L, Wolfgang M, Dickersin K. 2013. Defining race/ethnicity and explaining difference in research studies on lung function. European Respiratory Journal 41 (6) 1362-1370; DOI: 10.1183/09031936.00091612

44. Brottman, M. R., Char, D. M., Hattori, R. A., Heeb, R., & Taff, S. D. 2020. Toward Cultural Competency in Health Care: A Scoping Review of the Diversity and Inclusion Education Literature. Academic medicine : journal of the Association of American Medical Colleges, 95(5), 803–813. https://doi.org/10.1097/ACM.0000000000002995

45. Brown, F. W., Bryant, S. E., & Reilly, M. D. (2006). Does emotional intelligence as measured by the EQ-i – influence transformational leadership and/or desirable outcomes? Leadership & Organization Development Journal, 27(5), 330-351.

46. Bruce CA. 2002; The grief process for patient, family, and physician. J Am Os-teopath Assoc. 102(9 Suppl 3):S28-32.

47. Cameron, K., & Quinn, R. 2011. Diagnosing and changingorganizational culture: Based on the competing valuesframework (3ed Ed.). San Francisco, CA: Jossey-Bass.

48. Carr, S. E., Celenza, A., Mercer, A. M., Lake, F., & Puddey, I. B. (2018). Predicting performance of junior doctors: Association of workplace based assessment with demographic characteristics, emotional intelligence, selection scores, and undergraduate academic performance. Medical Teacher, 40(11), 1175–1182. https://doi.org/10.1080/0142159X.2018.1426840

49. Cassano F, et al 2020. Evaluation of Emotional Intelligence among Master's Degree Students in Nursing and Midwifery: A Cross-Sectional Survey. International journal of environmental research and public health, 17(17), 6347. https://doi.org/10.3390/ijerph17176347

50. Chan K, Petrisor B, Bhandari M. 2014. Emotional intelligence in orthopedic surgery residents. Can J Surg. 57(2):89-93.

51. Cherniss C, 2001: Emotional Intelligence and Organizational Effectiveness. In Cherniss, Cand Goleman, D (Eds). The Emotional Intelligent Workplace San Francisco, Jossey – Bass, pp.3 – 12.

52. Cherry MG, Fletcher,I Berridge D, O'Sullivan H. (2017) Do doctors' attachment styles and emotional intelligence influence patients' emotional expressions in primary care consultations? An exploratory study using multilevel analysis. Patient Education and Counseling 101 (2018) 659–664

53. Ciarrochi J, Dean FP, Anderson S. 2002. Emotional intelligence moderates the relationship between stress and mental health. Personality and Individual Differences. 32(2):197-209

54. Collier VU, McCue JD, Markus A, Smith L. 2002. Stress in medical residency: status quo after a decade of reform? Ann Intern Med;136(5):384–390

55. Conti & Holly. (2018) Multiple intelligences. Research Starters Education. p1-1. 12p.

56. Coskun, O., Ulutas, I., Budakoglu, I. I., Ugurlu, M., & Ustu, Y. (2018). Emotional intelligence and leadership traits among family physicians. Postgraduate medicine, 130(7), 644–649. https://doi.org/10.1080/00325481.2018.1515563

57. Coskun, O., Ulutas, I., Budakoglu, I. I., Ugurlu, M., & Ustu, Y. (2018). Emotional intelligence and leadership traits among family physicians. Postgraduate Medicine, 130(7), 644–649. https://doi.org/10.1080/00325481.2018.1515563

58. Costa H, Saavedra F, and Fernandes HM. 2021. 'Emotional Intelligence and Well-being: Associations and Sex- and Age-effects During Adolescence'.: 275 – 282.

59. Crawford P, Brown B, Tischler V, Baker C. 2010; Health humanities: the future of medical humanities? Mental Health Review Journal. 17;15(3):4-10.

60. Cross TL, Bazron BJ, Dennis KW, Isaacs MR. 1989. Towards A Culturally Competent System of Care, Volume I. Washington, DC: Georgetown University Child Development Center, CASSP Technical Assistance Center, 1989. [ISBN 9993938149]

61. D. Goleman, R. Boyatzis 2008, Social intelligence and the biology of leadership Harv Bus Rev, 86 (9) pp. 74-81 [136]

62. D. Goleman. 1998 What makes a leader? Harv Bus Rev, 76 (6) pp. 93-102

63. Davidson, R. J., Jackson, D. C., and Kalin, N. H. (2000). Emotion, plasticity, context, and regulation: perspectives from affective neuroscience. Psychol. Bullet. 126, 890–909. doi: 10.1037/0033-2909.126.6.890

64. Dermawan, A. (11 September 2021) Covid-19 situation in Penang worrying. News Straits Times. Retrieved from https://www.nst.com.my/news/nation/2021/09/726303/covid-19-situation-penang-worrying

65. Domnariu, C., Cernuşcă-miţariu, M., & Boitan, M. 2013. Organizational Culture – Important Factor In Delivering High Quality Health Care. Metalurgia International, 18 (8), 5-7.

66. Drame, I., Wingate, L., Unonu, J., Turner, M., Taylor, M. D., Bush, A., Jarvis, M., & Cawthorne,

T. A. 2021. The association between students' emotional intelligence, cultural competency, and cultural awareness. Currents in pharmacy teaching & learning, 13(9), 1146–1152. https://doi.org/10.1016/j.cptl.2021.06.030]

67. Dubey, R., Bryde, D. J., Blome, C., Roubaud, D., & Giannakis, M. (2021a). Facilitating artificial intelligence powered supply chain analytics through alliance management during the pandemic crises in the B2B context. Industrial Marketing Management, 96, 135–146. https:// doi. org/ 10. 1016/j.indma rman.2021.05 003

68. Dubey, R., Bryde, D. J., Foropon, C., Tiwari, M., Dwivedi, Y., & Schiffling, S. (2021b). An investigation of information alignment and collaboration as complements to supply chain agility in humanitarian supply chain. International Journal of Production Research, 59(5), 1586–1605. https:// doi. org/ 10. 1080/ 00207 543. 2020. 18655 83

69. Dugan JW, Weatherly RA, Girod DA, Barber CE, Tsue TT. 2014. A longitudinal study of emotional intelligence training for otolaryngology residents and faculty. JAMA Otolaryngol Head Neck Surg. 140(8):720-726.

70. Eslinger, P. J. 1998. Neurological and neuropsychological bases of empathy. European neurology, 39, 193-199

71. Espinosa, A., & Rudenstine, S. 2020. The contribution of financial well-being, social support,

and trait emotional intelligence on psychological distress. The British journal of clinical psychology, 59(2), 224–240. https://doi.org/10.1111/bjc.12242

72. Faye A et al, 2011. Study of emotional intelligence and empathy in medical postgraduates. Indian J Psychiatry. 53:140-44. 10.4103/0019-5545.82541

73. Fernandez-Berrocal P, Cabello R, Castillo R, Extremera N. 2012. Gender differences in emotional intelligence: The mediating effect of age. Psicol Conductual 20:77.

74. Fernández-Berrocal, P., and Extremera, N. 2008. A review of trait meta-mood research. Int. J. Psychol. Res. 2, 39–67

75. Gardner, L, and Stough C, (2002) Examining the relationship between Leadership and Emotional intelligence in senior level managers, Leadership &Organization Development Journal, 23(2) 68 – 8

76. General Medical Council, Tomorrow's Doctors, General Medical Council, London, 2021.

77. Gifford BD, Zammuto RF, Goodman EA. 2002: The relationship between hospital unit culture and nurses' quality of work life. J Healthc Manag, 47(1):13-25.

78. Goh K & Tey NP (2018) Personal income in Malaysia: Distribution and differentials. Economics Bulletin 38(2): 973-982

79. Goleman D. Emotional intelligence. New York: Bentham Books; 1995.

80. Goleman, D. 1998. Working with Emotional Intelligence.

81. Goleman, D., Boyatzis, R. & McKee, A. 2002. Primal Leadership: Realizing the Importance of Emotional Intelligence, Harvard Business School Press

82. González Castillo, A.R., Lizardo Vega Villanueva, E., Núñez Torreblanca, R., & Delgado Benites, F.J. 2013. Competencias interculturales y competencias emocionales en los estudiantes deciencias sociales y turismo de la universidad nacional José Faustino Sánchez Carrión. Retrieved from http://docplayer.es/7799190-Ministerio-de-educacion-superior-republica-decuba.html#show_full_text

83. Goodman EA, Zammuto RF, Gifford BD 2001: The competing values framework: Understanding the impact of organizational culture on the quality of work life. Organization Development Journal, 19(3):58

84. Griffith CH, Wilson JF, Langer S, Haist SA. 2003. House staff nonverbal communication skills and standardized patient satisfaction. J Gen Intern. Med;18(3):170-4

85. Guntersdorfer I, Golubeva I. 2018. Emotional Intelligence and Intercultural Competence: Theoretical Questions and Pedagogical Possibilities, Intercultural Communication Education, Volume 1 No. 2, https://dx.doi.org/10.29140/ice.v1n2.60

86. Gutiérrez-Cobo MJ, Cabello R, Fernández-Berrocal P. 2017. The Three Models of Emotional Intelligence and Performance in a Hot and Cool go/

no-go Task in Undergraduate Students. Frontiers in Behavioral Neuroscience. 11:33. doi=10.3389/fnbeh.2017.00033

87. Hajibabaee, F., A Farahani, M., Ameri, Z., Salehi, T., & Hosseini, F. 2018. The relationship between empathy and emotional intelligence among Iranian nursing students. International journal of medical education, 9, 239–243. https://doi.org/10.5116/ijme.5b83.e2a5

88. Haralur, S. B., Majeed, M. I., Afzal, M., & Chaturvedi, S. 2019. Association of sociodemographic factors and emotional intelligence with academic performance in clinical and preclinical dental courses. Nigerian journal of clinical practice, 22(8), 1109–1114. https://doi.org/10.4103/njcp.njcp_37_19

89. Helfrich CD, Li Y, Mohr DC, Meterko M, and Sales AE. 2007. Assessing an organizational culture instrument based on the Competing Values Framework: Exploratory and confirmatory factor analyses. Implementation Science 2007, 2:13 (1-14) doi:10.1186/1748-5908-2-13

90. Horvat L, Horey D, Romios P, Kis-Rigo J. 2014, Cultural competence education for health professionals. Cochrane Database of Systematic Reviews Issue 5. Art. No.: CD009405. doi: 10.1002/14651858.CD009405.pub2.

91. Hosseini, M., Elias, H., Krauss, S. E., & Aishah, S. (2010). A review study on spiritual intelligence, adolescence and spiritual intelligence: Factors that may contribute to individual differences in spiritual

intelligence and the related theories. Journal of Social Sciences, 6(3), 429–438.

92. Hutchison, B., J. Abelson, and J. Lavis. 2001. "Primary Care in Canada: So Much Innovation, So Little Change." Health Affairs 20 (3): 116–31.

93. Imran N, Aftab MA, Haider II, Farhat A 2013. Educating tomorrow's doctors: A cross sectional survey of emotional intelligence and empathy in medical students of Lahore. Pak J Med Sci; 29(3):710-714. doi: http://dx.doi.org/10.12669/pjms.293.3642

94. Issue V, Tomar R. 2016; A Study of Emotional Intelligence among Doctors. 5:303–8.

95. J. Campinha-Bacote. 2002. The process of cultural competence in the delivery of healthcare services: a model of care J Transcult Nurs, 13 (3), pp. 181-184 discussion 200-201

96. Jacobs, N., Huldtgren, A. 2021. Why value sensitive design needs ethical commitments. Ethics Inf Technol 23, 23–26. https://doi.org/10.1007/s10676-018-9467-3

97. Johnstone MJ, Kanitsaki O. 2006. Culture, language, and patient safety: making the link. International Journal for Quality in Health Care;18(5):383-8.

98. K. Barzykowski, A. Majda, P. Przyłęcki, M. Szkup. 2019. The cross-cultural competence inventory: validity and psychometric properties of the polish adaptation PLoS One, 14 (3)), Article e0212730, 10.1371/journal.pone.0212730

99. Kaur, D., Sambasivan, M. and Kumar, N. 2013, Effect of spiritual intelligence, emotional intelligence, psychological ownership and burnout on caring behaviour of nurses: a cross-sectional study. J Clin Nurs, 22: 3192-3202. https://doi.org/10.1111/jocn.12386

100. Khoo et al, 2017. Emotional exhaustion is associated with work related stressors: a cross-sectional multicenter study in Malaysian public hospitals. Arch Argent Pediatr. 115(3);212-219. doi.10.5546/aap.2017.eng.212

101. King, D. B., & DeCicco, T. L. 2009. A viable model and self-report measure of spiritual intelligence. International Journal of Transpersonal Studies, 28, 68–85.

102. Knazik SR, Gausche-Hill M, Dietrich AM, Gold C, Johnson RW, Mace SE, et al. 2003; The death of a child in the emergency department. Annals of Emer-gency Medicine. 42(4):519-529.

103. Koohbanani, Dastjerdi, Vahidi, and Far. 2013. The Relationship Between Spiritual Intelligence and Emotional Intelligence with Life Satisfaction Among Birjand Gifted Female High School Students. Procedia - Social and Behavioral Sciences 84 (2013) 314 – 320

104. Lee JY, McFadden KL, Lee MK, Gowen CR, 2021. U.S. hospital culture profiles for better performance in patient safety, patient satisfaction, Six Sigma, and lean implementation, International Journal of Production Economics, Volume 234,

108047, ISSN 0925-5273,https://doi.org/10.1016/j.ijpe.2021.108047.

105. Levenson, M. R., Aldwin, C. M., & Yancura, L. 2006. Positive emotional change: mediating effects of forgiveness and spirituality. Explore (New York, N.Y.), 2(6), 498–508. https://doi.org/10.1016/j.explore.2006.08.002

106. Lin D, Liebert CA, Tran J, Lau JN, & Salles A. 2016. Emotional intelligence as a predictor of resident well-being. J Am Coll Surg. 223(2):352–358

107. Lin H, et al 2017. Analysis on relationship of chronic fatigue and mental health of medical staff in Zhuhai City. Ind Health Occup Dis. 43(2):140–4. 148

108. Liu L, Xu P, Zhou K, Xue J, & Wu H. 2018. Mediating role of emotional labor in the association between emotional intelligence and fatigue among Chinese doctors: a cross-sectional study. BMC Public Health. 18:881 https://doi.org/10.1186/s12889-018-5817-7

109. Liu, L., Xu, P., Zhou, K., Xue, J., & Wu, H. 2018. Mediating role of emotional labor in the association between emotional intelligence and fatigue among Chinese doctors: a cross-sectional study. BMC Public Health, 18(1), 881. https://doi.org/10.1186/s12889-018-5817-7

110. Lopes PN, Grewal D, Kadis J, Gall M, Salovey P. 2006. Evidence that emotional intelligence is related to job performance and affect and attitudes at work. Psicothema. 18(Suppl):132–8

111. Madahi ME, Javidi N, Samadzadeh M 2013. The Relationship between Emotional Intelligence and Marital Status in Sample of College Students, Procedia - Social and Behavioral Sciences, Volume 84, Pages 1317-1320, ISSN 1877-0428, https://doi.org/10.1016/j.sbspro.2013.06.749.

112. Maguire P & Pitceathly C. 2002. Key communication skills and how to acquire them, Br. Med. J. 325 (7366) 697–700

113. Mahran SM. 2016. Using the Competing Value Framework Model for Developing an Organizational Culture Profile in Governmental Hospitals. American Journal of Nursing Science. Vol. 5, No. 6, pp. 288-294. doi: 10.11648/j.ajns.20160506.18

114. Martins, N., & Coetzee, M. 2007. Organisational culture, employee satisfaction, perceived leader emotional competency and personality type: An exploratory study in a South African engineering company. South African Journal of Human Resource Management, 5 (2), 20-32.

115. Matthew G, Zeidner M. 2001. Emotional intelligence, adaptation to stressful encounters and health outcomes. In: Bar-On R, Parker JDA, editors. The handbook of emotional intelligence. San Francisco, CA: Jossey-Bass/Pfeiffer;

116. Mayer JD, Roberts RD, Barsade SG. 2008. Human abilities: emotional intelligence. Annu Rev Psychol. 59:507–36.

117. Mayer, J. D., Caruso, D. R., and Salovey, P. 2016. The ability model of emotional intelligence:

principles and updates. Emot. Rev. 8, 290–300.doi: 10.1177/1754073916639667

118. Mayer, J. D., Roberts, R. D., and Barsade, S. G. (2008a). Human abilities: emotional intelligence. Annu. Rev. Psychol. 59, 507–536. doi: 10.1146/ annurev.psych.59. 103006.093646

119. Mayer, J. D., Salovey, P., and Caruso, D. 2002. Mayer-Salovey-Caruso Emotional Intelligence Test (MSCEIT) User's Manual Test. Toronto, ON: Multi-Health Systems

120. Mayer, J. D., Salovey, P., and Caruso, D. R. (2008b). Emotional intelligence: new ability or eclectic traits? Am. Psychol. 63, 503–517. doi: 10.1037/0003-066X.63. 6.503

121. Mayer, J. D., Salovey, P., Caruso, D. R., and Sitarenios, G. (2001). Emotional intelligence as a standard intelligence. Emotion 1, 232–242. doi: 10.1037/1528-3542.1.3.232

122. Mayer, J.D., and Salovey, P. (1997). "What is emotional intelligence?," in Emotional Development and Emotional Intelligence: Educational Implications, eds P. Salovey and D. Sluyter (New York, NY: Basic Books), 3–31.

123. McClelland L, Holland J, Lomas JP, Redfern N, Plunkett E. 2017. A national survey of the effects of fatigue on trainees in anaesthesia in the UK. Anaesthesia. 72(9):1069–77.

124. McCrae RR, Costa PT Jr., Ostendorf F, Angleitner A, Hrebícková M, Avia MD, et al. 2000. Nature over

nurture: Temperament, personality, and life span development. J Pers Soc Psychol 78:173-86.

125. McKinley SK 2014: The emotional intelligence of resident physicians. Doctoral dissertation, Harvard Medical School, Cambridge, MA

126. McKinley SK et al. 2015. A multi-institutional study of the emotional intelligence of resident physicians. Am J Surg.2015; 209(1):26-33.

127. Merz, E. L., et al 2014. Validation of Interpersonal Support Evaluation List-12 (ISEL-12) scores among English- and Spanish-speaking Hispanics/Latinos from the HCHS/SOL Sociocultural Ancillary Study. Psychological Assessment, 26(2), 384–394. https://doi.org/10.1037/a0035248

128. Miguez-Torres, N., Martínez-Rodríguez, A., Martínez-Olcina, M., Miralles-Amorós, L., & Reche-García, C. 2021. Relationship between Emotional Intelligence, Sleep Quality and Body Mass Index in Emergency Nurses. Healthcare (Basel, Switzerland), 9(5), 607. https://doi.org/10.3390/healthcare9050607

129. Mitra, S., Sarkar, A. P., Haldar, D., Saren, A. B., Lo, S., & Sarkar, G. N. (2018). Correlation among perceived stress, emotional intelligence, and burnout of resident doctors in a medical college of West Bengal: A mediation analysis. Indian Journal of Public Health, 62(1), 27–31. https://doi.org/10.4103/ijph.IJPH_368_16

130. Mitra, S., Sarkar, A. P., Haldar, D., Saren, A. B., Lo, S., & Sarkar, G. N. (2018). Correlation among

perceived stress, emotional intelligence, and burnout of resident doctors in a medical college of West Bengal: A mediation analysis. Indian Journal of Public Health, 62(1), 27–31. https://doi.org/10.4103/ijph.IJPH_368_16

131. Moshe Zeidner, Gerald Matthews, & Richard D. Roberts. (2009). What We Know About Emotional Intelligence : How It Affects Learning, Work, Relationships, and Our Mental Health. Bradford Books.

132. Naranjo-Valencia, J.C., Jimenez-Jimenez, D. and Sanz-Valle, R. 2016, "Studying the links between organizational culture, innovation, and performance in Spanish companies", Network of Scientific Journals from Latin America, Vol. 48 No. 1, pp. 30-41.

133. Nazia J, Dawood N, Sadaf M, Zil-e H, and Kanwal F. 2020. Impact of Spiritual Intelligence and Happiness on Mental Health among Adults. Ilkogretim Online - Elementary Education Online, 2020; Vol 19 (Issue 4): pp.4321-4327 http://ilkogretim-online.org doi: 10.17051/ilkonline.2020.04.764838

134. Nikolaou I, Tsaousis I. 2002. Emotional intelligence in the workplace: Exploring its effects on occupational stress and organizational commitment. Int JOrgan Analysis 10: 327–42.

135. Nunnally JC, Bernstein IH. 1994. Psychometric Theory. 3rd edition. New York, NY, McGraw-Hill Inc.;.

136. O'Donnell EP, Humeniuk KM, West CP, Tilburt JC. 2015; The effects of fatigue and dissatisfaction on how physicians perceive their social responsibilities. Mayo Clin Proc. 90(2):194–201.

137. O'Connor P J., Hill A, Kaya M, Martin B. 2019. The Measurement of Emotional Intelligence: A Critical Review of the Literature and Recommendations for Researchers and Practitioners. Frontiers in Psychology; 10. DOI=10.3389/fpsyg.2019.01116.

138. Ogunyemi D, Mehta S, Turner A, Kim D, Alexander C. 2014. Emotional intelligence characteristics in a cohort of faculty, residents, and medical students. J Reprod Med. 59(5-6):279-284.

139. Ostroff C, Kinicki AJ, Tamkins MM 2003. Organizational culture and climate. In Handbook of psychology: Volume 12, Industrial and organizational psychology Volume 12. Edited by: Borman WC, Ilgen DR, Klimoski RJ. New York, Wiley :565-587.

140. Papanagnou, D., Linder, K., Shah, A., London, K. S., Chandra, S., & Naples, R. (2017). An assessment of emotional intelligence in emergency medicine resident physicians. International journal of medical education, 8, 439–445. https://doi.org/10.5116/ijme.5a2e.a8b4

141. Pérez-González J, Saklofske DH, Mavroveli S. 2020. Trait Emotional Intelligence: Foundations, Assessment, and Education. Frontiers in Psychology; 11. DOI=10.3389/fpsyg.2020.00608.

142. Placek, S. B., Franklin, B. R., & Ritter, E. M. (2019). A Cross-Sectional Study of Emotional Intelligence in Military General Surgery Residents. Journal of Surgical Education, 76(3), 664–673. https://doi.org/10.1016/j.jsurg.2018.10.013

143. Podila SP 2018; emotional intelligence and income-a case study. Int. J. of Adv. Res. 6 (Dec). 282-288] (ISSN 2320-5407). www.journalijar.com

144. Psilopanagioti A, Anagnostopoulos F, Mourtou E, Niakas D. 2012. Emotional intelligence, emotional labor, and job satisfaction among physicians in Greece. BMC Health Serv Res. 12:463.

145. Psilopanagioti A, Anagnostopoulos F, Mourtou E, Niakas D. 2012. Emotional intelligence, emotional labor, and job satisfaction among physicians in Greece. BMC Health Serv Res; 12: 463. 10.1186/1472-6963-12-4633541956

146. Puliyakkadi S et al 2020. Dimensions of emotional intelligence of doctors in a tertiary care centre in kerala. 7(2) Page: 48-51

147. Punia N, Dutta J, Sharma Y. (2015). Emotional intelligence. A Theoretical Framework. International Journal of Scientific & Engineering Research, Volume 6, Issue 5; 967-1006.

148. Rahman MS, Ferdausy S, and Uddin MA. 2012. Exploring the Relationships between Emotional Intelligence, Leadership Styles and Gender: An Empirical Study. SIU Journal of Management, Vol.2, No.2. ISSN: 2229-0044

149. Ranasinghe P, Wathurapatha W, Mathangasinghe Y, Ponnamperuma G. 2017. Emotional intelligence, perceived stress and academic performance of Sri Lankan medical undergraduates. BMC Med Educ 17(1): 41e47.

150. Ranasinghe, P., Senadeera, V., Gamage, N. et al. 2020. Temporal changes in emotional intelligence (EI) among medical undergraduates: a 5-year follow up study. BMC Med Educ 20, 496. https://doi.org/10.1186/s12909-020-02404-x

151. Ranasinghe, P., Wathurapatha, W. S., Mathangasinghe, Y., & Ponnamperuma, G. (2017). Emotional intelligence, perceived stress and academic performance of Sri Lankan medical undergraduates. BMC medical education, 17(1), 41. https://doi.org/10.1186/s12909-017-0884-5

152. Ravikumar R, Rajoura O P, Sharma R, et al. 2017. A Study of Emotional Intelligence Among Postgraduate Medical Students in Delhi. Cureus 9(1): e989. DOI 10.7759/cureus.989

153. Razia B. and Nabi Ahmad 2017. Emotional intelligence and Socio-economic Status as the determinants of Academic achievement among Adolescents, International Journal of Education and Psychological Research (IJEPR) Volume 6, Issue 2,137-142.

154. Reker, G. T. 1997. Personal meaning, optimism, and choice: Existential predictors of depression in community and institutional elderly. The Gerontologist, 37, 709–716.

155. Robinson, M. R., Thiel, M. M., Shirkey, K., Zurakowski, D., & Meyer, E. C. 2016. Efficacy of training interprofessional spiritual care generalists. Journal of palliative medicine, 19(8), 814-821.

156. Rodrigues, N., & Rebelo, T. (2022). The bandwidth dilemma applied to trait emotional intelligence: Comparing the contribution of emotional intelligence factor with its facets for predicting global job satisfaction. Current Psychology, 41(4), 2218–2226. https://doi.org/10.1007/s12144-020-00740-1

157. Rose DM, et al. 2017. Associations of fatigue to work-related stress, mental and physical health in an employed community sample. BMC Psychiatry. 17(1):167.

158. Sabanciogullari S., Çatal N., & Doğaner F. (2019). Comparison of Newly Graduated Nurses' and Doctors' Opinions About Spiritual Care and Their Emotional Intelligence Levels. https://doi.org/10.1007/s10943-019-00760-7

159. Sadeghniiat-Haghighi K, Yazdi Z. 2015. Fatigue management in the workplace. Ind Psychiatry J. 24(1):12–7.

160. Sadovyy, M, Sanchez-Gomez, M. & Breso, E. 2021. COVID-19: How the stress generated by the pandemic may affect work performance through the moderating role of emotional intelligence. Pers Individ Dif. 180: 110986. doi: 10.1016/j.paid.2021.110986.

161. Salles A, Liebert CA, Greco RS. 2015. Promoting balance in the lives of resident physicians: a call to action. JAMA Surg. 150(7):607-608.

162. Salovey P, Mayer JD. Emotional intelligence. Imagin Cogn Pers. 1990;9(3): 185–211.

163. Sancoko, R., Setiawan, M., & Troena, E. 2019. The influence of organizational culture and spiritual intelligence on employee performance through emotional intelligence. MEC-J (Management and Economics Journal), 3(1), 67-80. doi:https://doi.org/10.18860/mec-j.v0i2.5510

164. Sataloff, R. T, 2020. Emotional Intelligence and Physician Wellness. Ear, Nose & Throat Journal, 99(3), 157–158. https://doi.org/10.1177/0145561319827721

165. Satterfield J, Swenson S, Rabow M. (2009). Emotional intelligence in internal medicine residents: Educational implications for clinical performance and burnout. Ann Behav Sci Med Educ; 14:65-8.

166. Schernhammer ES, Colditz GA. 2004. Suicide rates among physicians: a quantitative and gender assessment (meta-analysis). Am J Psychiatry.;161(12):2295–2302

167. Schim SM, Doorenbos AZ, Miller J, Benkert R. 2003. Development of a Cultural Competence Assessment Instrument. Journal of Nursing Measurement, Volume I I, Number 1

168. Schimmack, U. (2008). "The structure of subjective wellbeing," in The Science of Subjective Well-Being. eds M. Eid and R. J. Larsen (New York, NY: Guilford), 97–123.

169. Schutte NS, Malouff JM, and Bhullar N. 2009. The Assessing Emotions Scale. Springer.

170. Schutte, N. S., Malouff, J. M., Thorsteinsson, E. B., Bhullar, N., and Rooke, S. E. 2007. A meta-analytic investigation of the relationship between emotional intelligence and health. Pers. Individ. Dif. 42, 921–933. doi: 10.1016/j.paid.2006.09.003

171. Schutte, N. S., Schuettpelz, E, & Malouff, J. M. (2001). Emotional intelligence and task performance. Imagination, Cognition, and Personality, 20, 347-354

172. Schutte, N.S., Malouff, J.M., Hall, L.E., Haggerty, D.J., Cooper, J.T., Golden, C.J., & Dornheim, L. (1998). Development and validation of a measure of emotional intelligence. Personality and Individual Differences, 25, 167-177.

173. Schutte, N.S., Price, I., & Malouff, J.M. (2007). Situational aspects of emotional intelligence. Manuscript in preparation.

174. Scott T, Mannion R, Davies H, Marshall M. 2003. The Quantitative Measurement ofOrganizational Culture in Health Care: A Review of the Available Instruments. HSR: Health Services Research 38:3 (923-945)

175. Seeleman C, Suurmond J, Stronks K. 2009; Cultural competence: a conceptual framework for teaching and learning. Med Educ. 43(3):229–37.

176. Serebrakian AT, Petrusa ER, McKinley SK, Ortiz R, Austen WG, Phitayakorn R. 2021. Evaluating and Comparing Emotional Intelligence and Improvement Mindset of Plastic Surgery Residents. J Surg Res.:S0022-4804(21)00445-5. doi: 10.1016/j.jss.2021.06.061. Epub ahead of print. PMID: 34399991.

177. Shahid, R., & Adams, W. 2020. Emotional Intelligence Level Higher in Residents Who Took a Gap Year Before Medical School. Advances in medical education and practice, 11, 559–562. https://doi.org/10.2147/AMEP.S268464

178. Shahin M. A. 2020. Emotional intelligence and perceived stress among students in Saudi health colleges: A cross-sectional correlational study. Journal of Taibah University Medical Sciences, 15(6), 463–470. https://doi.org/10.1016/j.jtumed.2020.09.001

179. Shanafelt TD, Balch CM, Bechamps GJ, et al. 2009. Burnout and career satisfaction among American surgeons. Ann Surg.;250(3): 463–471.

180. Sharp, G., Bourke, L. and Rickard, M.J.F.X. 2020, Review of emotional intelligence in health care: an introduction to emotional intelligence for surgeons. ANZ Journal of Surgery, 90: 433-440. https://doi.org/10.1111/ans.15671

181. Shirom A. (2003). Job-related burnout: A review. In: Quick JC, Tetrick LE, editors. Handbook of Occupational Health Psychology. Washington, D.C.: APA;p. 245-64.

182. Shortell SM, et al 1995. Assessing the impact of continuous quality improvement/total quality management: concept versus implementation. Health Services Research 30(2):377-401

183. Singh, S. K. (2007). Role of emotional intelligence in organisational learning: An empirical study. Singapore Management Review, 29(2), 55-74.

184. Snowden, A et al. 2015,The relationship between Emotional Intelligence, previous caring experience and mindfulness in student nurses and midwives: A cross sectional analysis. Nurs. Educ. Today 35, 152–158.

185. Stami, T., Ritin, F., & Dominique, P. 2018. Demographic predictors of emotional intelligence among radiation therapists. Journal of medical radiation sciences, 65(2), 114–122. https://doi.org/10.1002/jmrs.277

186. Strote J, Schroeder E, Lemos J, Paganelli R, Solberg J, Range Hutson H. 2011. Academic emergency physicians' experiences with patient death. Acad Emerg Med.;18:255-260.

187. Subramanian, I.D., & Yen, C.L. 2013. Emotional intelligence of leaders and organizational culture: Evidence from IT companies in Malaysia. African Journal of Business Management, 7, 882-890.

188. Tarba, S.Y., Ahammad, M.F., Junni, P., Stokes, P. and Morag, O. 2019, "The impact of organizational culture differences, synergy potential, and autonomy granted to the acquired high-tech firms on the M&A performance", Group and Organization Management, Vol. 44 No. 3, pp. 483-520

189. Tellegen, A. 1991. Personality traits: Issues of definition, evidence, and assessment. In D. Cicchetti & W. M. Grove (Eds.), Thinking clearly about psychology: Essays in honor of Paul E. Meehl, Vol. 1. Matters of public interest; Vol. 2. Personality and psychopathology (pp. 10–35). University of Minnesota Press.

190. Thoits PA. 2011. Mechanisms linking social ties and support to physical and mental health. J Health Soc Behav. 52:145-161

191. Thomas G. 2021. Research Methodology and Scientific Writing. 2nd Ed. Springer Nature.

192. Thomas NK. (2004). Resident burnout J.AMA; 292:2880-9.

193. Thørrisen, M. M., Sadeghi, T., & Wiers-Jenssen, J. 2021. Internal Consistency and Structural Validity of the Norwegian Translation of the Ten-Item Personality Inventory. Frontiers in psychology, 12, 723852. https://doi.org/10.3389/fpsyg.2021.723852

194. Topaloglu A.O. 2014. The study of college students' emotional intelligence qualities, Social and Behavioral Sciences 152 1274 – 1281.

195. Toscano-Hermoso MD et al, 2020. Emotional Intelligence and Its Relationship with Emotional

Well-Being and Academic Performance: The Vision of High School Students. Children (Basel, Switzerland), 7(12), 310. https://doi.org/10.3390/children7120310

196. Ugoani J. 2015 Emotional Intelligence and Organizational Culture Equilibrium – A Correlation Analysis. J A Social Sci Humanities 2015, 1:1, 36-47, Available at SSRN: https://ssrn.com/abstract=2682000

197. Umeaku NN, Nnedum OAO, Nweke KO. 2021. The validation of the ten-item personality inventory (tipi) in the nigerian sample. Interdisciplinary Journal Of African & Asian Studies (IJAAS). 7(2).

198. Upadhyay, P. and Kumar, A. 2020, "The intermediating role of organizational culture and internal analytical knowledge beteen the capability of big data analytics and a firm's performance", International Journal of Information Management, Vol. 52, C, 102100, doi: 10.1016/j.ijinfomgt.2020.102100.

199. Wada K,et al, 2008. Factors on working conditions and prolonged fatigue among physicians in Japan. Int Arch Occup Environ Health; 82(1):59–66.

200. Walter O, Shenaar-Golan V & Routray S (2021) Cross-Cultural Comparison of How Mind-Body Practice Affects Emotional Intelligence, Cognitive Well-Being, and Mental Well-Being. Front. Psychol. 12:588597: 1-8. doi: 10.3389/fpsyg.2021.588597

201. Warrier U, Shankar A, & Belal HM (2021). Examining the role of emotional intelligence as a

moderator for virtual communication and decision making effectiveness during the COVID-19 crisis: revisiting task technology fit theory. Annals of Operations Research. https://doi.org/10.1007/s10479-021-04216-8

202. Watt, K., Abbott, P. & Reath, J. 2016. Developing cultural competence in general practitioners: an integrative review of the literature. BMC Fam Pract 17, 158 https://doi.org/10.1186/s12875-016-0560-6

203. Weinberger, L. A. (2002). Emotional intelligence: Review & recommendations for human resource development research and theory. Proceedings of the Annual Academy of Human Resource DevelopmentConference, 1006-1013.

204. Weng HC et al. 2011. Associations between emotional intelligence and doctor burnout, job satisfaction and patient satisfaction. Med Educ.45(8):835–42.

205. Weng HC, Chen HC, Chen HJ, Lu K, Hung SY 2008: Doctors' emotional intelligence and the patient doctor relationship. Med Educ. 42:703-11. 10.1111/j.1365-2923.2008.03039.x

206. Weng HC, Hung CM, Liu YT, Cheng YJ, Yen CY, Chang CC. 2011. Associations between emotional intelligence and doctor burnout, job satisfaction and patient satisfaction. Med Educ; 45; 8: 835-842. 10.1111/j.1365-2923.2011.03985.x

207. Weng, H.-C., Hung, C.-M., Liu, Y.-T., Cheng, Y.-J., Yen, C.-Y., Chang, C.-C., & Huang, C.-K. (2011). Associations between emotional intelligence

and doctor burnout, job satisfaction and patient satisfaction. Medical Education, 45(8), 835–842. https://doi.org/10.1111/j.1365-2923.2011.03985.x

208. Wigglesworth C. 2011. Spiritual Intelligence and Why It Matters. Deep Change, Inc

209. Williams, T. H., & Griffin, C. H. 1967. Income Definition and Measurement: A Structural Approach. The Accounting Review, 42(4), 642–649. http://www.jstor.org/stable/244159

210. Wilson-Stronks A, Lee KK, Cordero CL, Kopp AL, Galvez E. 2008. One Size Does Not Fit All: Meeting The Health Care Needs of Diverse Populations. Oakbrook Terrace, IL: The Joint Commission, 2008

211. Wirtz MR. 2019. It's written all over your face : examining the relationship between socioeconomic status and empathic accuracy. University of Richmond UR Scholarship Repository Honors Theses.

212. Xenikou, A. and Simosi, M. 2006, "Organizational culture and transformational leadership as predictors of business unit performance", Journal of Managerial Psychology, Vol. 21 No. 6, pp. 566-579.

213. Yebra Delgado, S., García Faza, V., Sánchez Calvo, A., Suárez Gil, P., & González Gómez, L. 2020. Relación entre la inteligencia emocional y el burnout en los médicos de Atención Primaria [Relationship between emotional intelligence and burnout syndrome in Primary Healthcare doctors]. Semergen, 46(7), 472–478. https://doi.org/10.1016/j.semerg.2020.02.006

214. Yildirim-Hamurcu, S & Terzioglu, F (2021) Nursing students' perceived stress: Interaction with emotional intelligence and self-leadership. Perspect Psychiatr Care. doi: 10.1111/ppc.12940.

215. Zeb, A. et al. 2021 "The competing value framework model of organizational culture, innovation and performance", Business Process Management Journal, Vol. 27 No. 2, pp. 658-683. https://doi.org/10.1108/BPMJ-11-2019-0464

216. Zeidner M, Hadar D, Matthews G, Roberts RD 2013, Personal factors related to compassion fatigue in health professionals. Anxiety Stress Coping. 26:595-609. 10.1080/10615806.2013.777045

217. Zohar, D., & Marshall, I. 2000. Spiritual intelligence: The ultimate intelligence. London: Bloomsbury Publishing.

218. Wicks, J., Nakisher, S., & Grimm, L. (2021). Emotional intelligence (EI). Salem Press Encyclopedia of Health

219. Zhang, L., Roslan, S., Zaremohzzabieh, Z., Jiang, Y., Wu, S., & Chen, Y. (2022). Perceived Stress, Social Support, Emotional Intelligence, and Post-Stress Growth among Chinese Left-Behind Children: A Moderated Mediation Model. International Journal of Environmental Research and Public Health, 19(3). https://doi.org/10.3390/ijerph19031851

220. Ciarrochi J., Deane F., Anderson S. 2002. Emotional intelligence moderates the relationship between stress and mental health. Pers. Individ. Differ. 32: 197-209. 10.1016/S0191-8869(01)00012-5

www.ingramcontent.com/pod-product-compliance
Lightning Source LLC
La Vergne TN
LVHW041130150826
845673LV00007B/2266

* 9 7 9 8 8 9 6 3 2 7 5 6 1 *